Program Authors

Diane August	Jan Hasbrouck
Donald R. Bear	Margaret Kilgo
Janice A. Dole	Jay McTighe
Jana Echevarria	Scott G. Paris
Douglas Fisher	Timothy Shanahan
David Francis	Josefina V. Tinajero
Vicki Gibson	

McGraw Hill Education

Cover and Title pages: Nathan Love

www.mheonline.com/readingwonders

Send all inquiries to:
McGraw-Hill Education
2 Penn Plaza
New York, NY 10121

ISBN: 978-0-07-678835-4
MHID: 0-07-678835-0

Printed in the United States of America.

2 3 4 5 6 7 8 9 RMN 20 19 18 17 16

A

Unit 5 Wonders of Nature

The Big Idea: What kinds of things can you find growing in nature?

? Essential Question

What do living things need to grow?

Go Digital!

Watch It Grow!

COLLABORATE

Talk About It

How can you care for a garden?

Say the name of each picture.

1

2

Read each word.

3   **hop**   **ham**   **hip**

4   **hot**   **hid**   **him**

Read Together

my

Do you like **my** hat?

It is hot in **my** garden.

7

Hop Can Hop!

I am Dot.
I like Hop.

I am hot.
See **my** hat on top!

Hop is hot.
Hop can hop on top.

Hop can hop, hop, hop.

I can hop, hop, hop!

Jan Bryan-Hunt

13

I can sit.
Hop can sit.

Jan Bryan-Hunt

Pop and I can sip.
Hop can sip.

15

Write About the Text

Hop Can Hop!

I am Dot.
I like Hop.

Pages 8–15

Amanda

I responded to the prompt: **Write a story. Tell what a make-believe pet and its owner can do.**

Student Model: *Narrative Text*

Characters
Ella and Harry are the characters in my story.

Harry and Me

I am Ella.

I like Harry.

Harry likes to play ball.

Order

I told my ideas about Ella and Harry in an order that makes sense.

I throw a ball to Harry.

He jumps up to catch it.

We have lots of fun!

Grammar

The word **I** is a **pronoun.** It takes the place of the name Ella.

Your Turn

COLLABORATE

Write a story telling about what you and your make-believe pet can do at the lake.

Go Digital!
Write your response online.
Use your editing checklist.

17

Weekly Concept Trees

Essential Question

How do living things change as they grow?

Go Digital!

Growing Tall

Talk About It

How will this tree change?

Ee

Say the name of each picture.

1

2

Read each word.

3 **Ed**   **pet**   **ten**

4 **den**   **net**   **met**

Read Together

are

Ted and Ed **are** friends.

The branches **are** bare.

Ed and Ned

Ed is not a pet.
Ned is not a pet.

Ned is up, up, up.
See Ned! See Ned!

Ed met Ned.
Ned met Ed.

Ed can sip, sip, sip.
Ned can sip, sip, sip.

Annie Katz/Photographer's Choice/Getty Images

Are Ed and Ned hot?
Are Ed and Ned wet?

27

Ed can hop, hop, hop.

Ned can nap, nap, nap.

Write About the Text

Ed and Ned

Ed is not a pet.
Ned is not a pet.

Pages 22–29

Charlie

I responded to the prompt: **Would it be better for Ed and Ned to do things together or to do things alone? Why do you think so?**

Student Model: *Opinion*

I think it is better for
Ed and Ned to do things
together.
It is more fun.
Ed and Ned work together.

Clues
I used the photos to understand what Ed and Ned do.

Topic

All of my sentences tell about Ed and Ned.

Ed and Ned swim together.

They are a team.

Ed and Ned are happy together.

I think they are better together.

Grammar

The word **I** is a **pronoun.** It is used in place of the name Charlie.

COLLABORATE

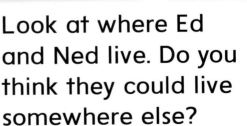

Your Turn

Look at where Ed and Ned live. Do you think they could live somewhere else? Why or why not?

Go Digital!
Write your response online.
Use your editing checklist.

Weekly Concept Fresh from the Farm

Farm Fresh

COLLABORATE

Talk About It

What food do you see?

 Ff

 Rr

Say the name of each picture.

1

2

Read each word.

3 fin   fed   fan

4 rip   rat   rod

| **he** | **with** |

He picked a red apple.

I go **with** Ron to the farm.

Ron With Red

Ron is **with** Red.
Red is a pet.

Chris Lensch

Red can see a  bird.

Can Ron see it on top?

Dad can see ten .

oranges

He can fit ten in a .

basket

Red can see a  bird.

Can Ron see it on top?

Chris Lensch

Mom can see ten .

tomatoes

Mom can fit ten on top.

Ron can sit and sip.

Red can see a .
bird

Ron did not see a .
bird

Red can see it on top!

Chris Lensch

Write About the Text

Pages 36–43

Pedro

I responded to the prompt: **Write a journal entry from Ron's point of view about his day. Use the illustrations and text in the story.**

Clues

I used clues in the photos to figure out where they went.

Grammar

The word **I** is a **pronoun.**

Student Model: *Narrative Text*

Today I went to a farm with my family.

We brought my dog Red.

First, Dad picked oranges.

Order

I told the events in the order
in which they happened.

Next, Mom picked tomatoes.
Red and a bird became
friends.
Last, we went home.

Your Turn

Write a journal entry
from Red's point of
view about his day
at the farm. Use the
illustrations and text
in the story.

Go Digital!
Write your response online.
Use your editing checklist.

45